CELEBRATING THE NAME KATHLEEN

Celebrating the Name Kathleen

Walter the Educator

Copyright © 2024 by Walter the Educator

All rights reserved. No part of this book may be reproduced in any manner whatsoever without written permission except in the case of brief quotations embodied in critical articles and reviews.

First Printing, 2024

Disclaimer
This book is a literary work; poems are not about specific persons, locations, situations, and/or circumstances unless mentioned in a historical context. This book is for entertainment and informational purposes only. The author and publisher offer this information without warranties expressed or implied. No matter the grounds, neither the author nor the publisher will be accountable for any losses, injuries, or other damages caused by the reader's use of this book. The use of this book acknowledges an understanding and acceptance of this disclaimer.

dedicated to everyone with the first name of Kathleen

KATHLEEN

In lands where the sun meets the sea,

KATHLEEN

There dwells a name, a melody, Kathleen,

KATHLEEN

A symphony of syllables woven with grace,

KATHLEEN

Inscribed in the hearts of time and space.

KATHLEEN

Kathleen, oh Kathleen, a name so divine,

KATHLEEN

A tapestry of dreams, where stars entwine,

KATHLEEN

Each letter a whisper, a gentle breeze,

KATHLEEN

That dances through forests, across the seas.

KATHLEEN

In gardens of wonder, where flowers bloom,

KATHLEEN

Kathleen's name enchants, dispelling gloom,

KATHLEEN

For in its essence, there lies a tale,

KATHLEEN

Of strength, of beauty, that shall never pale.

KATHLEEN

From ancient hills to modern streets,

KATHLEEN

Kathleen's name resounds, a rhythm sweet,

KATHLEEN

It echoes in laughter, in tears it weeps,

KATHLEEN

A treasure trove of memories it keeps.

KATHLEEN

In the hush of night, beneath the moon's soft gleam,

KATHLEEN

Kathleen's name lingers, a celestial theme,

KATHLEEN

It sings of love, of passion's fire,

KATHLEEN

Of dreams that soar, ever higher.

KATHLEEN

With every heartbeat, with every breath,

KATHLEEN

Kathleen's name whispers of life and death,

KATHLEEN

It weaves through the fabric of destiny,

KATHLEEN

A timeless echo of eternity.

KATHLEEN

In tales of old, in legends bold,

KATHLEEN

Kathleen's name shines like burnished gold,

KATHLEEN

It graces the lips of bards and seers,

KATHLEEN

A beacon of hope through the years.

KATHLEEN

So let us raise our voices high,

KATHLEEN

In praise of Kathleen, beneath the sky,

KATHLEEN

For in her name, we find our song,

KATHLEEN

A melody sweet, forever strong.

KATHLEEN

In the gentle kiss of morning's light,

KATHLEEN

Kathleen's name blooms, a flower bright,

KATHLEEN

It paints the dawn with hues so fair,

KATHLEEN

A promise of joys beyond compare.

KATHLEEN

In the realm of dreams, where fantasies roam,

KATHLEEN

Kathleen's name guides, leading us home,

KATHLEEN

Through realms of imagination, where wonders unfold,

KATHLEEN

In Kathleen's embrace, we find stories untold.

KATHLEEN

ABOUT THE CREATOR

Walter the Educator is one of the pseudonyms for Walter Anderson. Formally educated in Chemistry, Business, and Education, he is an educator, an author, a diverse entrepreneur, and he is the son of a disabled war veteran. "Walter the Educator" shares his time between educating and creating. He holds interests and owns several creative projects that entertain, enlighten, enhance, and educate, hoping to inspire and motivate you.

Follow, find new works, and stay up to date with Walter the Educator™
at WaltertheEducator.com

www.ingramcontent.com/pod-product-compliance
Lightning Source LLC
LaVergne TN
LVHW012052070526
838201LV00082B/3940